BEST OF ENEMIES

BY **MARK ST. GERMAIN**

BASED ON *THE BEST OF ENEMIES*
BY OSHA GRAY DAVIDSON

★

★

DRAMATISTS
PLAY SERVICE
INC.

AUTHOR'S NOTE

BEST OF ENEMIES, suggested by the book by Osha Gray Davidson, is the true story of the relationship of black civil rights activist Ann Atwater and C.P. Ellis, Exalted Cyclops of the Ku Klux Klan. Fueled by the hatred they felt for each other, Ellis and Atwater faced off as co-chairpersons of a committee formed to debate school desegregation in Durham.

BEST OF ENEMIES exposes the poison of prejudice through Atwater and Ellis who, by confronting their hatred, discover the real enemy they share.

BEST OF ENEMIES received its world premiere at Barrington Stage Company (Julianne Boyd, Artistic Director; Tristan Wilson, Managing Director) in Pittsfield, Massachusetts, on July 21, 2012. It was directed by Julianne Boyd; the set design was by David M. Barber; the costume design was by Kristina Lucka; the lighting design was by Scott Pinkney; the sound design was by Brad Berridge; and the production stage manager was Michael Andrew Rodgers. BEST OF ENEMIES was sponsored by Sydelle and Lee Blatt. The cast was as follows:

C.P. ELLIS	John Bedford Lloyd
ANN ATWATER	Aisha Hinds
BILL RIDDICK	Don Guillory
MARY ELLIS	Susan Wands

BEST OF ENEMIES was subsequently presented at George Street Playhouse, in New Brunswick, New Jersey, opening on November 30, 2012. It was directed by Julianne Boyd; the set design was by David M. Barber; the costume design was by Kristina Lucka; the lighting design was by Scott Pinkney; the sound design was by Brad Berridge; and the production stage manager was Thomas Clewell. The cast was as follows:

C.P. ELLIS	John Bedford Lloyd
ANN ATWATER	Aisha Hinds
BILL RIDDICK	Don Guillory
MARY ELLIS	Susan Wands

CHARACTERS

C.P. ELLIS — Exalted Cyclops of the Durham Ku Klux Klan. White.

MARY ELLIS — Wife of C.P. White.

ANN ATWATER — Civil rights activist and civic leader. Black.

BILL RIDDICK — College educated, community organizer. Black.

TIME

1971.

PLACE

Durham, North Carolina.

BEST OF ENEMIES

April 4, 1968.

Pre-show, recording of "Stand Up and Be Counted" by National Knights of the Ku Klux Klan.

KLAN MEMBERS.
> *Stand up and be counted*
> *Show the world that you're a man*
> *Stand up and be counted*
> *Go with the Ku Klux Klan*
> *We are a sacred brotherhood who love our country too*
> *We always can be counted on when there's a job to do*
> *We serve our homeland day and night*
> *When there's a job to do*
> *And proudly wear our robes of white*
> *Protecting liberty*

C.P. Come on, boys! I can't hear you!

ALL.
> *Stand up and be counted*
> *Show the world that you're a man*
> *Stand up and be counted*
> *And join the Ku Klux Klan*

C.P. One bullet! One bullet, that's all it took! Right here, through his jaw, down his spine and he dropped like a monkey from a tree! Truth is, boys, I was a little sad they killed him. *(Angry shouting.)* Hold on, now! I'm sad he never made it here to Durham next week or we could'a done the job ourselves! *(Laughter.)* Here's to the gunman who shot Martin Lucifer Coon! *(C.P. raises his beer as fellow Klansmen cheer. Lights down on Klavern as the sound of the cheer blends with the sounds of a crowd's protest chant.)*

CROWD. *(Offstage.)*
> *We shall not, we shall not be moved*
> *We shall not, we shall not be moved*
> *Just like a tree that's standing by the water*
> *We shall not be moved*
> *Black and white together, we shall not be moved*
> *Black and white together, we shall not be moved*
> *We shall not, we shall not be moved*
> *Just like a tree that's standing by the water*
> *We shall not be moved*
> *We're fighting for our children, we shall not be moved*
> *We're fighting for our children we shall not be moved*
> *Just like a tree that's standing by the water*
> *That's planted by the water*
> *We shall not be moved*

(Lights up on Ann Atwater facing an unseen receptionist at the Durham town hall. She is a veteran warrior for civil rights.)

ANN. Put down that phone! Yes, you heard me! And don't touch it again when I'm talking to you! How much of Durham do you want to see burn down tonight? We are not a mob, we are citizens who demand to see our mayor, and not some pissant councilman! You tell the Mayor Ann Atwater wants him down here now to tell us how he's going to lower the flag, close the schools and explain how this city plans to honor Doctor King. Now pick that phone up and dial. And if you call the police you'll be talking on your way out that window. *(Lights down on Ann as we hear the sound of a car driving into a gas station and the "ring" of the gas station's line as it drives over it. May, 1971. Lights up on the gas station of C.P. Ellis. There is a radio on the cash register desk next to a stand of motor oil and a Confederate flag and pictures beside it, including an 1867 picture of KKK member and Civil War hero Nathan Bedford Forster in Confederate uniform. Bill Riddick, a black man in his thirties wearing a jacket and tie, enters the gas station and listens. He holds a clutch of flyers.)*

RADIO ANNOUNCER. On the third anniversary of the death of Martin Luther King, Joe Etha Collier, an eighteen-year-old black girl, was shot dead in broad daylight coming out of a sweet shop with her classmates in her hometown of Drew, Mississippi. Drew High School has been recently desegregated. *(Bill turns up the radio as C.P. Ellis enters behind him, wiping oil off his hands with a rag.)* A white farm worker was put under arrest only 4 hours later. It is suspected that a county voter drive aided by Civil Rights volunteers from the North escalated racial tensions. Joe Etha Collier was known as a good student and Drew High School's champion sprinter.

C.P. Not fast enough. Turn off my radio and wipe the dial. I don't want your germs on it.

BILL. *(Catching the cloth, he looks at C.P. and smiles. Nothing deters him.)* Good morning. I'm here to invite you to a meeting next Tuesday night. It's our first to discuss the problem of school desegregation.

C.P. I can solve that problem right now. You people stay in your own schools.

BILL. That is definitely a solution to consider.

C.P. *(Not the reaction he expected.)* Who are you?

BILL. Bill Riddick. I'm a community organizer.

C.P. "Community organizer." Does that make you a Commie or a union boy, boy?

BILL. I'm from the Department of Education. We have a grant to create programs addressing racial issues in our schools. The process is called a "charrette."

C.P. A "charrette."

BILL. It's French for meetings between people of different points of view to come to an understanding, and we keep meeting 'til they do. *(Hands him flyer.)*

C.P. Well, don't this beat all. You talk French, drive a nice new car and dress like you're wearing a white man costume on Halloween. I can't wait to go down to your "charrette"; we'll all hold hands and sing "Dixie." *(Crumbles up invitation.)* Now wipe off my dial and get out before I call the police. Looks to me like you're about to steal it.

BILL. We both know how much violence there's been in Durham. Don't you want to stop it?

C.P. I will. As soon as I get my city back. The dial.

BILL. Lot of oil on this cloth; your hands must be filthy, Mr. Ellis.

C.P. You know who I am, do you?

BILL. C.P. Ellis. Exalted Cyclops of the Ku Klux Klan, Lodge Nine, Durham Klavern. Rumor is, you also sell the finest white lightning in the county and store it in that grease pit —

C.P. *(Takes a tire iron from behind the counter, slams it down.)* You get your black ass off my property, nigger, while you can still walk.

BILL. We meet Tuesday, 8 P.M., at the YMCA. Hope to see you

there. *(Tosses rag to C.P. and exits. C.P. goes to the phone and dials.)*
C.P. *(On phone.)* Denny, it's C.P. You call us an emergency meeting ... Tonight, that's when. Seven o'clock. Tell anybody who can't come they better give me a damn good reason. *(Lights down on C.P., as lights reveal Ann entering her living room with Bill.)*
BILL. Can we sit down?
ANN. You won't be here that long. You know what the Good Book says is the greatest sin?
BILL. Not reading the Good Book?
ANN. Pride. Pride opens the door to every other sin there is.
BILL. You think I'm prideful?
ANN. Either that or your mama dropped you on your head as a baby.
BILL. Huh, she always told me that was an accident. School segregation's been against the law for years. It's about time Durham faces that.
ANN. Face it? We've been living it. Police shooting black students just for sitting out front of their dormitory. Us burning down the Housing Authority and so many stores the mayor called in the National Guard. We've had more folks die than you've had birthdays and you think you can come down here from the North, and make Durham give a damn about any laws but our own?
BILL. Actually, I'm from North Carolina, too.
ANN. Where?
BILL. Hartford County.
ANN. That's still north of here.
BILL. Mrs. Atwater, everyone's tells me you're an important leader in this community. We need you at this meeting.
ANN. But unlike you, I'm not being paid to be there. All I'd get out of it is high blood pressure and a sore throat from shouting things I've shouted all my life. I'll save my strength for cleaning up after you're gone.
BILL. I just met C.P. Ellis.
ANN. Sweet Jesus. Then get to church and dunk yourself in holy water. I see that man every time I walk a picket line. If looks could kill, there wouldn't be a black face left in town.
BILL. I invited him to the charrette.
ANN. You are a damn fool. Since C.P. Ellis took charge, the Klan's grown so big they built a new hall twice the size of the old one. He also started a Youth Klan to start poisoning the children early. And

that man doesn't just hate, he wants to kill. Last year, one of his baby Klanners got his bus money stolen off him by a couple of black boys downtown by the Sears. There's nothing in this world that could have made C.P. Ellis happier. He filled his car with guns and rednecks and went hunting. He found some black men standing on the corner, just down the street here. When Ellis shouted, "Where were you niggers today?" my neighbor Lincoln King yelled right back, "Who you calling 'niggers'?" Ellis opened fire. Lincoln would be dead today if that cracker could shoot straight. That's the man you invited. And he's going to pack the place with more like him.

BILL. That's why I need people there who aren't afraid of them.

ANN. I'm not afraid of anybody. But when I see a snake I don't talk to it, I cut its head off.

BILL. I hear there are people afraid of you. They call you "Roughhouse Annie," don't they? Roughhouse Annie who can "kill anybody who wasn't already dead."

ANN. That's me.

BILL. Mrs. Atwater, if I didn't know any better I'd say that's a smile full of pride. *(Lights down on Bill and Ann.)*

KLANSMAN. *(In darkness.)* Let us bow our heads in prayer. *(Lights slowly rise, revealing in shadows a Klansman robed in red leading the Klavern's prayer. Behind him, the banner: "UNITED KLANS OF AMERICA, UNIT 9.")*

KLANSMAN and KLAN MEMBERS. Our Father, God of Life and Liberty, we humbly thank Thee for opening the eyes of all good people to the evil which has been forced upon us. Help us to overcome our enemies, and give our hearts the courage to destroy these agents of Satan. We ask this in the name of Thy Son, Christ Jesus, Amen. *(Lights fully up, C.P. removes his hood and addresses the membership.)*

C.P. You all heard the government's trying to make Hillside High into darkie heaven. I got a call today from Councilman Nash, you know Ferris, and he wants us to go to their meeting. I said, "Ferris, I do not intend to associate with a bunch of niggers or nigger lovers." But Ferris said he needs us. If we don't go, who's going to be there but niggers and whites who hate their own race? We are the last patriots. We've got to protect our wives and children. So I'm thinking, this, this is no meeting, it's a goddamn war. We fight now for what we know is right or before you say "spade" they'll be in our classrooms sniffing after our daughters. Now I want to hear from you. *(Shouts from Klan members blends into sound of applause. As lights are fading.)* All right. Now that's more like it! *(Lights up on the YMCA. There are several metal chairs set up. Ann sits in one of them, her large pocketbook in her lap. Bill addresses the group, the meeting already in progress.)*

BILL. Thank you, Mayor. And we've got Councilman Nash, Howard Clement from the Black Solidarity Committee and Joe Becton from the City's Human Relations Commission to thank for helping to organize the next few weeks. We're here to communicate. That means we're here to say everything we feel. But we're here to listen, too. So let's get to work. Tonight I want to start by asking you one question, just one: What are the problems in Durham schools? *(Silence.)* Any at all. *(Silence.)* There's none? *(C.P. enters, stands by the door, hesitating about going in. Ann spots him; they lock eyes.)* All right, then, tell me this: Are there any problems here in Durham, period. *(Silence.)* Really. Well I guess I'd better move here to Durham. *(Ann rises.)*

ANN. You know there's problems and everybody in this room knows it, too. *(To all in room.)* What's wrong with you people? The only thing that's happened here in the 17 years since Brown v. the Board of Education is a committee to "study the problem" and somebody setting fire to East End Elementary. The "colored" school. So what did our City Council do? There was plenty of room in their white schools, but they decided to run East End on split shifts so they could keep their kids safe from ours. The problem's white racism and it always will be!

C.P. The problem's that we've been too good to niggers! The problem's letting the federal government tell us what to do!

ANN. The problem is stupid crackers like C.P. Ellis!

C.P. Me? Look around this room if you want to see stupid. Look at the hair on these people; it's like they got big black bushes growing off their heads! And there — grown men wearing beads and ladies' circus blouses.

ANN. Everybody knows they're called dashikis, and they are part of our heritage.

C.P. Then go back to Africa! That's your heritage! They want to look different because even they know they are different. We let them have their marches and protests and they expect us to lay down and roll over like we did with the Jews and the Catholics and the commie unions? *(To All.)* When are we going to have the guts to say, "What

12

about the white man?" You got the courts looking out for you. They can get up in their schools and cuss the white man, but do you think our schools will let me into an assembly to tell kids about the KKK so they can hear the truth for once? Hell no! The truth is that whites and niggers will never get along because they shouldn't. I say no more wasting time like we're doing tonight.

BILL. *(Applause, but when it stops Bill continues applauding heartily.)* Now that's more like it!

ANN. What the hell does that mean?

BILL. He hates us. He doesn't hide it and he's got the courage to say it to our faces. I think we're off to a good start. We're going to split into smaller groups now, but first let's take a break so Mrs. Atwater and Mr. Ellis can build up another head of steam. *(Sounds of chairs being pushed back. Low, surprised conversation. Bill approaches C.P.)* Mr. Ellis, I'm glad you're here. *(Bill puts out his hand for C.P. to shake; C.P., disgusted, stares at it then walks out. Ann approaches Bill.)*

ANN. You think you're smarter then everybody in this room, don't you?

BILL. That's hard to tell yet; we just got started.

ANN. Here's some "honesty." I don't like you, Riddick. You think you're Jesus Christ coming to town on Palm Sunday and I think you're the ass he rode in on.

BILL. Mrs. Atwater. This is what I love about a charrette. A person can speak whatever's on their mind.

ANN. I always say, you scratch a white man and you find a bigot. Why do I think that if I scratched your skin I'd find a white man? *(Ann leaves. Lights out on Bill, lights rise on the dark parking lot, as Ann walks across it.)*

C.P. *(Offstage.)* Atwater! *(She stops. C.P. emerges from the shadows, a machine gun in hand.)* Just want you to know: this goes where I go. *(C.P. steps into the light.)*

ANN. Let me show you something. *(Ann reaches into her purse; C.P., alarmed, raises the gun. Ann pulls out a Bible.)* This is my grandmother's Bible. You take that gun out one more time and I'll knock the hell out of you with it.

C.P. Maybe you should read that Bible instead. Slavery is a Biblical right, you know that? You can buy slaves and sell them, men, women and kids. You can use them however you want and if they don't remember their place you can beat them dead. "Slaves obey your masters, with respect and fear." *(Points at her Bible.)* It's all in there.

ANN. Maybe you should keep reading. Being a slave had nothing to do with skin color. It was all about money. Slaves were slaves because they had none, and the folks who bought them did.

C.P. Jesus never said a word against it.

ANN. Jesus said, "The Son of Man did not come to be a slave master but a slave who will give his life to rescue many people." What I want to know, Ellis, is why you give a damn what Jesus thought, when if he walked through your Klan door today you'd string him up 'cause he's a Jew. *(Lights down on Ann and C.P., up on Bill in his motel room.)*

BILL. *(On phone.)* The director please, it's Bill Riddick. *(Pause.)* Don't you worry; he'll want to take this call. *(Pause.)* Jack; Bill. We're off to a good start here ... Then you heard wrong ... Maybe they think of it as name-calling. I call it getting acquainted. Jack, you tell the boys in Washington they're in good hands. *(Lights up on C.P. in kitchen.)*

C.P. *(On phone with Councilman Ferris Nash.)* I don't know what this Riddick's up to. He didn't bat an eye at a word I said, then he wanted me to shake his hand! He's making a damn fool of himself.

BILL. This is my third charrette; did you send me here because I don't get the job done? I'm not calling for backup, I'm calling because I have an idea. *(Pause.)* I'm going to tell you! But you better sit down first.

C.P. We don't need to throw a wrench into their damn meetings, Ferris. They're going to screw things up just fine all by themselves. There's no sense going back there.

BILL. Maybe it sounds crazy, but you know what? This is going to be the biggest success we ever had or a world–class catastrophe — and either one is going to put segregation on every television in this country. *(Lights up on Ann, on phone.)*

ANN. Ellis is crazy dangerous and I wouldn't trust Riddick in a shithouse with a muzzle.

BILL. You know me, Jack. I can sell snowflakes in a blizzard. *(Lights down on Bill.)*

C.P. Hell, I know you trust me, Ferris. All right, you want me to keep an eye on things, then I'll do it. You tell the boys at City Hall not to worry. We'll come down so hard on those spear chuckers they'll want to hang their own selves. *(Lights down on C.P. Lights up on Ann's apartment.)*

ANN. Hey, hey, hey! Don't you dare raise your voice to me, Anita, when you never said one single word at the charrette! You can go back tomorrow night, but I'm done. *(Hangs up; phone rings again.)* What do you want now? *(Lights up on Bill.)*

BILL. I want to know the best place in town to have lunch tomorrow.

ANN. Ruth's Café, East Fourth, a block from the courthouse.

BILL. What time would be good for you?

ANN. The day you leave town.

BILL. That's what C.P. Ellis thought you'd say.

ANN. Ellis?

BILL. I have a proposal I want to make to both of you.

ANN. Are you telling me C.P. Ellis said he'd sit down and eat with us?

BILL. You don't want to miss that. He could choke to death right in front of you. *(Lights down on Ann; lights up on C.P. in the kitchen, the phone ringing.)*

C.P. C.P.

BILL. Mr. Ellis, this is Bill Riddick. I'd like to buy you lunch tomorrow.

C.P. I don't eat watermelon. *(Hangs up; calls offstage.)* Mary! Are we eating tonight or what? *(Mary Dixon Ellis enters.)*

MARY. You want to heat it up and set the table or go change Larry? Take your pick. *(Phone rings; both look at it.)*

C.P. It could be important.

MARY. So are we. *(Looks offstage.)* Timmy, leave your brother alone! That's dangerous! *(Phone rings again; C.P. looks to Mary.)* Come on, C.P. Let's remind the kids what eating like a family looks like. *(Phone rings.)*

C.P. Might be the Mayor.

MARY. Might be the President. Either one will call back. *(Phone rings; C.P. goes to it.)*

C.P. I'll make it fast. *(He grabs the phone as Mary exits.)*

MARY. Take your time. Or better yet, why don't just you invite everybody over? Maybe one of them will change Larry.

C.P. Yeah?

BILL. It's Bill again, Mr. Ellis. We must have been disconnected.

C.P. We were, by me.

BILL. Everybody I talk to tells me you've got friends in high places in this town. I've got an idea that I think you all would be interested in.

C.P. What is it?

BILL. I'll tell you all about it in Ruth's Café, tomorrow at one.

C.P. You're a funny one, Billy; I'll give you that. But I don't eat with porch monkeys.

BILL. I don't think the powers that be would want you to miss what I have to say. Don't let them down. One o'clock. Good night, now. *(Bill hangs up; C.P. slams down the phone.)*

C.P. Don't anybody pick up this damn phone! *(Lights down on C.P. Sound of restaurant noise, conversations, silverware clanking and a hit from 1971 is on the radio. Lights up on Ruth's Café. Ann and Bill are seated with plates full before them and a third plate for C.P. C.P. enters and spots Ann but talks only to Bill.)*

BILL. Mr. Ellis!

C.P. You never said she'd be here!

ANN. *(To Bill, suspicions confirmed.)* Is that right?

BILL. You're a little late, Mr. Ellis, so we ordered for you. Sit down; your pork chops are getting cold. And they are delicious.

C.P. *(Looks around him.)* This is like a zoo; everybody staring like we're animals.

BILL. Sooner you sit, the sooner you're out of here.

C.P. The whole town's gonna know I'm talking to you.

ANN. *(To Bill.)* That cracker doesn't realize I'm the one who's going to look like Aunt Jemima.

BILL. Tell *him* that.

C.P. I'm the one they'll tar and feather.

BILL. Tell her.

ANN. Tell that fool I'll get the tar.

C.P. Say what you've got to say, Riddick, or I'm walking.

BILL. All right, then. I want the two of you to co-chair the charrette. *(Both are stunned.)*

C.P. What?

ANN. You *were* dropped on your head.

C.P. You think I'd work with that pile of pig shit?

ANN. *(Rising.)* Shut your mouth, you son of a bitch, or I'll slap it off your face! *(They shout over each other.)*

C.P. You threaten me again and you'll regret that day you were born —

ANN. What you need is a brain, Ellis, not a gun —

BILL. *(Interrupts.)* SIT DOWN! Everybody's looking at you.

16

(Pause. Both sit.)

C.P. Is this a joke, Riddick? There's no way I'd do that and you know it.

ANN. You think I'm some fool for you or the whiteys you work for?

BILL. No. I think you're both smart enough to realize change is coming, and both of you want it to be in your favor.

ANN. You're a hell of a talker but you're saying nothing.

C.P. These are our problems. You want to change things? Go to New York City or California. I've lived here all my life. We know what's right and wrong and the way things should stay.

BILL. But they won't stay the same; they'll just keep getting worse. I think both of you can look past your own egos and understand what this charrette's really about. Not you, not white or black, but the best education for your children. *(To C.P.)* You want that, don't you?

C.P. Of course I do.

BILL. *(To Ann.)* And you want the same?

ANN. I want equal education.

BILL. So get it. Or tell me somebody else in this city you trust to get it for you. Give me their names and I'll call them right now. Then you can go home and see what they do for your kids. Or they don't. You can change this whole town. Co-chair the charrette and make sure that what changes is best for you. Maybe not by miles, maybe by just a foot, or an inch.

C.P. You are dumber than a bag of hammers. *(He rises.)* I'm done here. *(He takes out his wallet.)*

BILL. Lunch is on me.

C.P. I don't take nothing from nobody. Especially one of you. *(C.P. throws money on the table and exits.)*

ANN. *(To Bill.)* You're paying for mine. *(Lights down on café. In darkness, a cigarette is lit. Lights up on C.P. and Mary's kitchen. Mary sits at the table with a cup of coffee, smoking. Sound of door opening and closing. C.P. enters, all energy.)*

C.P. You're still up?

MARY. I'm still up. *(During C.P.'s venting, Mary sits quietly, watching him and smoking.)*

C.P. You're not going to believe what just happened. I'm driving home and I stopped at the light on Dean and South? This long–haired kid, white, too, pulls up alongside, looks over with a big

17

smile and does this to me — *(He gives the "peace" sign.)* I jumped out of the car and before he can even get those fingers down, I punched him in the face, hard as I could. He just sat there bleeding when I drove away. Didn't even try coming after me. I'm telling you, this town is going crazy fast.

MARY. You want to know *why* I'm still up?

C.P. Guess I'm going to find out.

MARY. Timmy's all in a knot the same as you are. That Thompson boy down the street told him you were in the café today with two coloreds. He said, "Your daddy's a nigger lover."

C.P. That's crazy talk. I went there for Timmy and Vickie, to keep these pickaninnies from taking over our schools like they're doing this country. There's nineteen million of them out there now, you know that? Nineteen million and —

MARY. *(Overlapping.)* "Multiplying like black bunnies." I've heard it, C.P., I've heard it all. You're talking to yourself.

C.P. Nothing new there. I'm going to bed.

MARY. And tomorrow you'll get up, go to work, then go to another meeting where you boys can take turns cranking each other up with hate talk.

C.P. It's not about hate and you know it! The Klan's about love for our country and families.

MARY. So when are we going to see some of that Klan love? I've had it up to here, C.P. I'm getting Timmy and Vickie through school and getting Larry through every minute of the day. Washing him, dressing him, wiping him — a thirteen-year-old boy.

C.P. I know it's hard.

MARY. You're not here long enough to know. What are you running from, C.P.? *(Pause.)* We made Larry. *We* made him. And he needs a father who's not ashamed.

C.P. The hell I am!

MARY. Prove it. Take him out for a ride after work, just you and him. Go to the park. He loves the slide. Help him up the ladder and then hold on to his hand when he slides down. He laughs all the way, no matter how many times he does it.

C.P. Of course I'll take him. Just not tomorrow.

MARY. What is it this time?

C.P. The damn charrette. This Riddick, the new one they brought in? He's working some angle to turn Durham into coon town and who do you think people are counting on to stop them?

MARY. How could this city ever survive without you?

C.P. Are you done now?

MARY. Almost. *(She pulls up an empty bottle of bourbon from beside her chair.)* I found two of these. How many did I miss? *(He looks at her.)* I'm tired, C.P. I am so tired. *(Lights down on C.P. and Mary, lights up on Ann in her church, speaking with her unseen pastor.)*

ANN. Don't you tell me to turn the other cheek, nobody is gonna slap me again. Why should I work to put their little white racists in my schools? I will not waste another minute of my life, and you can call it hate or pride because I've got both in my heart. You want me to pray? I pray that C.P. Ellis burns in the hell he's made for me and every black man and woman in this city. Until then, Pastor, I will keep my knife right here so I can use it. *(Lights down on Ann. Sound of phone ringing; Ann enters her apartment and picks it up.)*

ANN. Hello.

C.P. This is C.P. Ellis.

ANN. *(Braced for anything.)* Uh-huh.

C.P. There's no way you and Riddick are going to get away with this.

ANN. Get away with what?

C.P. I'm going to co-chair this charrette.

ANN. Why would you do that?

C.P. To keep you all from taking over and turning this thing into a Sambo circus.

ANN. Are you crazy or stupid? You think I'd ever work with a bigot like you?

C.P. Atwater, that's the best news I've heard all day. *(C.P. hangs up; blackout. On a screen, a collage of civil rights protests. Jesse Helms' voice is heard.)*

JESSE HELMS. *(Voiceover.)* White people, wake up before it's too late. Crime rates and irresponsibility among Negroes are a fact of life, which must be faced. Denying that would be the same as trying to pretend that they do not have a natural instinct for rhythm and for singing and dancing.

ANNOUNCER. You've been listening to Jesse Helms on WRAL, 101.5, Durham. *(Lights up on Bill, C.P. and Ann seated at a long table. C.P. sits at one head, Ann at the other, Bill between them. C.P.'s wearing his garage work shirt, his name sewn over the pocket.)*

BILL. We need to come up with an agenda to bring to the steering committee; it will save us a lot of time. Either of you want to take notes?

C.P. I'm no secretary.

ANN. I can remember everything I need to.

C.P. Same here.

ANN. Oh really? Then why are you wearing a shirt with your own name sewn on it?

C.P. You want to keep flapping those bumper lips, then how 'bout you learn to say "with" instead of "wiff"?

BILL. I'll take notes. Do you have any suggestions on what to call our charrette?

ANN. That's what you called it.

BILL. A charrette's what it is, but that would be like calling it a town meeting. It's good to find a name that tells people what it's about.

ANN. Saving Our Schools. S.O.S.

BILL. Can't get more direct than that. C.P.?

C.P. We got a program in South Carolina called "Save Our Schools."

BILL. Who does?

C.P. The Klan.

BILL. Good to know. How about "Support Our Schools"?

ANN. I don't want to support them. I want to save them.

C.P. You want a Klan name, that's just fine with me.

BILL. Let's put it to the committee. Now we have to decide on a place to meet.

ANN. Can't we stay at the "Y"?

BILL. With all the nights we need, they can't accommodate us.

C.P. How 'bout the Civic Center?

BILL. I think it's too big, and there's no place to break down into small groups.

ANN. How about a church?

C.P. What church?

ANN. My church. First Baptist.

C.P. That's in the colored part of town. No whites are going to set foot into some Negro church.

ANN. Does God change color in your cracker church?

BILL. What about Harris Elementary? It has an auditorium, air conditioning and plenty of classrooms for small groups. Plus, it's right on the border of black and white neighborhoods.

C.P. That's a black school. I told you; we've got to meet someplace people want to go.

ANN. You mean where you want.

C.P. I mean someplace neutral.

ANN. Where's the gray section of town?

C.P. You hold it at Harris, you're telling every white man in this town not to come.

ANN. No, we're telling rednecks not to come.

C.P. Then change S.O.S. to "Save Our Spooks."

ANN. *(To Riddick.)* I will not sit here anymore with this pecker-wood.

C.P. No nigger's going to talk to me that way —

ANN. And no whitey's worth talking to!

BILL. Buckwheat, Massa, Jigaboo, Fishbelly, Knuckle Dragger, Ditch Pig, Rube, Ring Tail, Wonder Bread, Tar Baby, Whitey, Woolhead, Bubba, Jungle Bunny, Buckra, Blackie, Mayonnaise, Mandingo, Shit Kicker, Silverback, Pasty Face, Nigglet, Caveman, Cotton Picker, Ofay. You got more? *(Silence.)*

ANN. There's always more.

BILL. Can we move on now?

C.P. No point to it. We meet at Harris and nobody will go. Plain and simple.

BILL. It's your job to get them there. Knock on doors, pass out flyers, use your pull in the community and pack the place.

C.P. If we did pick Harris, who's going to protect the whites?

BILL. Protect them from what?

C.P. From the blacks. *(Pause. Bill and Ann are taken aback.)*

ANN. I'll protect you, C.P.

C.P. *(Annoyed, rising.)* I got to go to work.

ANN. *(Rises.)* I've got kids to feed. *(C.P. walks out first. Ann stops at the door, turns back to Bill.)* You still think this can work, do you?

BILL. Right now I'll consider it a success if you two don't kill each other.

ANN. Good luck with that. *(Sound of school bell; classes changing. Lights down on Ann, up on the office of Harris Elementary School. C.P. and Ann stand behind a counter, not speaking. Bill enters hurriedly carrying a stack of papers.)*

BILL. The copy machine's slow but you can start with these. If you can collate and staple we can pass them out tonight. I've got to find the custodian to unlock the auditorium, then I'll be back with more. *(He puts them on a table in front of Ann and C.P. with a sta-*

pler and leaves. What follows is a completely silent sequence. Both stare at the pile of papers divided into three — three pages to be collated and stapled together. Neither touches them — a waiting game. Ann finally reaches for them, taking one page from each pile, one, two, three, then slaps them down. One, two, three. One, two, three. One, two, three. She glares at C.P. When's he going to do anything? C.P. grabs the stapler and staples one set, two, then three and starts his completed pile. Ann continues sorting. C.P. continues stapling, grabbing sets from Ann the minute she makes them. The pace increases, neither still saying a word; papers slapped down like cards in a card game, the staple banged harder and harder until the entire pile is almost completed. It's funny until C.P. and Ann's hands brush together in grabbing papers. C.P. pulls back as if stung. Ann looks at him as he hurriedly wipes his hand on the side of his pants. C.P. meets her look of contempt as Bill enters, holding more papers and feels the silence.)

BILL. Everything all right?

ANN. Just fine.

C.P. You bet. *(Lights down on office. On screen, either a crawl of the following or a picture of a white working man sitting dejectedly on a park bench as narration is heard.)*

NARRATOR. You should have gotten that job, but it went to a minority because of Ted Kennedy's racial quotas. Is that right? Harvey Gantt says it is, that a man's skin color matters more than his abilities. Give him your opinion when you vote this Tuesday. For quotas, Harvey Gantt. For you, Jesse Helms. *(Lights up on the Harris Elementary auditorium. Ann and C.P. are at separate podiums, Bill sitting upstage between them. Ann addresses the crowd.)*

ANN. All in favor of "Save Our Schools," put your hands up. *(She does. She and C.P. see it's the majority.)* All opposed? *(Small response.)* All right then. We've got ourselves a name, S.O.S.

BILL. That's great, thank you, Ann. Now we'll hear from our co-chair, C.P. Ellis. *(Large applause. C.P. steps forward. He carries notes.)*

C.P. All right. We've got a bunch of committees we need you to volunteer for. All of you. In Room 201, we got the Student Survey Committee. We want to give one to every kid in our schools, white and black, and get their take on how things are now and how they want them to stay the same. *(Ann looks at him.)* Room 203, Parents' Survey. Same thing. We want to find out what everybody here wants, not Washington, D.C.

ANN. You want to just fill out all the surveys yourself?

C.P. What's that mean?

ANN. Why don't we wait to find out what everybody wants before you tell them.

C.P. That's what we're doing. Room 210's for a committee to look at the books used in all our grammar and high schools, white and black, and compare them. Go down to 210 and we'll get your names.

ANN. Everybody on the High School Book Committee should have graduated high school.

C.P. We didn't vote on that.

ANN. We didn't take a vote, everybody agreed.

C.P. Not that I heard.

ANN. Then you didn't listen.

C.P. You listen now. I didn't go to high school. I had to go to work after eighth grade. So you're saying my opinion doesn't matter?

ANN. Mine either. I dropped out in tenth. How's somebody going to compare high school history books when they never finished high school? We might as well get the opinion of a blind man.

(C.P. is about to explode. Bill quickly rises.)

BILL. C.P.?

C.P. *(To Ann.)* My boy Larry's blind.

ANN. *(Silence.)* I didn't know.

C.P. He's retarded, too. Make sure you tell everybody that.

ANN. I told you I had no idea.

C.P. Oh no?

BILL. Moving on. We'll be working some long days and nights so it would be good to have some refreshments when we take a break. Maybe even some entertainment at supper. We should have a committee for that. C.P., is there another room available?

C.P. *(Looking at his clipboard.)* Room 103. People can meet there.

BILL. Thank you. So if we could have some volunteers for Entertainment.

ANN. My church choir said they would come down and sing.

BILL. That would be nice.

C.P. What are we having for white folks?

ANN. You got a Klan choir?

C.P. *(Still simmering.)* I want to put up a Klan exhibit. Right here. For all you and for the kids, too. The history of the KKK.

BILL. Mr. Ellis —

C.P. Look around here at the bulletin boards in these hallways. You got your Martin Luther King posters and that peanut guy and a bunch of Negroes I never even heard of. I don't see a single white man except Abraham Lincoln. If that's not prejudice, tell me what is?

ANN. What do you want to put up? Pictures of men in sheets burning crosses?

C.P. Now that's an ignorant thing to say, which is why you need an education. Lighting crosses is a symbol of our faith in Jesus Christ, the Light of the World. And our robes and hoods go way back, all the way to the Middle Ages in Europe, where men had secret societies because they wanted their good deeds to be anonymous.

BILL. Mr. Ellis, I think it would be counterproductive to what we're trying to do here.

C.P. This is still a democracy, isn't it? I say let everybody here decide.

ANN. I say that if I can have my choir, he can have his Klan exhibit. *(Both C.P. and Bill are taken aback.)* Let's put it to a vote. *(To crowd.)* All in favor? That's it, then.

C.P. Well, all right then. *(C.P. exits.)*

BILL. OK, see you all tomorrow night. *(Follows Ann.)* Ann! What was that about?

ANN. I gave an inch. Isn't that what you wanted?

BILL. Letting him bring the Klan in? Are you serious? It will be a disaster!

ANN. Maybe.

BILL. Maybe you want it to be. And when it is, it's on your head, not mine! I'll tell the Committee, the newspapers and anybody who will listen it's your fault!

ANN. What's this really about, Riddick? Helping us or making you a hero?

BILL. You don't know the first thing about me. You think I'm some puppet you can blame when this whole thing explodes.

ANN. I'm going home.

BILL. You're hearing me out! You think you deserve a black martyr medal; nobody could have suffered like you!

ANN. *(Skeptical.)* And you did?

BILL. My daddy was a tenant farmer, here, in North Carolina. My mama cooked for the white family he picked peanuts for, and every night we sat on their back steps waiting for her to finish washing their dishes from dinner so we could go home and eat our own.

ANN. Nobody forced you to pick peanuts and wash dishes, did they?

BILL. Oh, no. I was too smart for that. I got work at the country club and told them I would *not* be a waiter. They gave me a job at the pool instead, right alongside the white boys. Except I was the only one who had to wear long pants because their members couldn't stand seeing black legs. So I said, I'm out of here. I enrolled at the University of Chapel Hill to get myself an education. I learned how white folks can eat their lunches real fast when a black man sits at their table. You know what's really magical? How apartments instantly fill up when a black man wants to rent one. You think I'm some Uncle Tom doing this for a paycheck, but I'm fighting for our people the same as you. Except what makes us different is that I'm not a hypocrite. I don't carry the Good Book around to say "this is who I am," because when I heard about the riots here in Durham, you weren't preaching the Good Book — you were throwing Molotov cocktails. *(Bill leaves. Ann stares after him. Blackout. Sound of school bell. Lights up on the Harris Elementary library. C.P. Ellis puts finishing touches on his KKK display: A table showcases Klan literature. Blow–up photographs on tripods show robed and hooded Klan members holding burning crosses in their hands. A reproduction of an old poster showing KKK members hanging white carpetbaggers. C.P. suddenly stops, hearing teen voices from the hallway. He looks out as the murmuring grows louder. Behind him, Ann enters, stopping at the sight of the burning crosses. C.P. turns to see her.)*

C.P. Those black kids out there. They're gonna come in here and trash our exhibit. I hear them talking. *(He starts to leave.)*

ANN. Where are you going?

C.P. To get my gun.

ANN. Hold on. *(Ann steps to the door and shouts down the corridor.)* Hey! HEY! That's right, all of you! You want to come in here and tear things up? Well that's not gonna happen! You're going back to class right now and tell them about this exhibit. Then you're going to bring them all back here and see these pictures and study every word you read. You want to know where a person's coming from, you've got to know how he thinks. Fight with your brain. Now get your friends and get right back here or I'm coming after you. You heard me, get! *(Ann turns back, finished. C.P. stares at her.)*

C.P. You've got one big mouth.

ANN. My daddy told me only white people talk quiet. We've got to talk louder to be heard. *(She picks up a flyer.)* My choir's singing tomorrow after supper. Are you coming or not?

C.P. They know any Klan songs?

ANN. I'd sure like to see you teach them. *(Blackout on library. Lights up on C.P. and Mary's kitchen. Mary's listening to a song on the radio as she wipes the table when C.P. rushes in, apoplectic.)*

C.P. MARY! Did you see my car? *(He points behind him through the door.)* Somebody filled my trunk with cement! Cement! Right to the top! My gun's in there! They buried my goddamn gun! Well I'm going out right now to get a bigger one and find out who the hell did it!

MARY. I did.

C.P. *(Pause, stunned.)* What?

MARY. I did it.

C.P. Why?

MARY. You told me you'd never use that gun again. But when I opened the trunk, there it was, loaded, too, in the trunk of the car our children ride in.

C.P. We've got the car keys! They couldn't touch it!

MARY. So it's fine, then. Just go out and shoot somebody else again, go to prison and leave your family to fend for themselves. What a good father you are!

C.P. *(Pause.)* Just how much do you hate me?

MARY. I don't know who's in that head of yours anymore to hate. You've changed, C.P.

C.P. So have you.

MARY. I hope I have! We got married when I was sixteen! You loved some girl who thought every word you said was Gospel, and I loved somebody who made me feel more special than I am. But I'm not that girl anymore. I'm a woman who can fill a car trunk with cement.

C.P. You're talking crazy.

MARY. I could be. I've been crazy enough to stay this long.

C.P. You want to go, then do it! Get out right now! Go on and leave!

MARY. I already did. So did you. So you tell me, C.P., do we have anything worth coming back to? *(Phone rings. C.P. doesn't move, staring at her.)*

C.P. I don't know. *(Lights down on Mary staring at C.P., not moving as we hear the sound of the New Generation Singers, Ann's choir. Lights up on school auditorium. Hymn: "I'm Going with Jesus.")*

> I'm going with Jesus all the way
> I'm going with Jesus all the way
> You can't stop me, you can't turn me

I'm going with Jesus all the way
(Lights up reveal Ann on a chair seated next to Bill. Ann loves the music and shows it. She sings along, sometimes shouting, "Yes, Lord!" "I'm going!" etc. Bill is more restrained. C.P. enters, arms crossed.)
Sometimes I have to fast and pray
Sometimes I have to steal away
Sometimes I have to cry out help me lord
(Oh yes)
(Ann is clapping along. Bill joins her. C.P. puts his hands in his pockets.)
I know if I hold my peace, the Lord will take care of me
I'm going to Jesus all the way
(C.P. takes his hands out of his pockets, clasps them before him.)
If you love Him, just clap your hands
(A little louder)
If you love Him, just clap your hands
(A little louder)
(Reflexively, C.P. starts to clap tentatively. He claps off the beat.)
If you need Him, just clap your hands
(A little louder)
Come on and just clap your hands
(A little louder)
I'm going, with Jesus
I'm going, with Jesus
I'm going with Jesus
(Ann turns, sees C.P. clapping. Seeing her, C.P. leaves.)
ANN. We're getting to him. Oh yeah, we're getting to him. *(Bill looks at her, not understanding. Lights down on auditorium as choir concludes.)*
CHOIR.
I'm going with Jesus
All the way
(Lights up on front porch of the Ellis home. Bill holds a box, Mary comes to the door.)
BILL. Hello, is this the Ellis residence?
MARY. It is.
BILL. I'd like to drop off these surveys for Mr. Ellis to distribute. I went to the gas station but it's closed.
MARY. He's at the bank. Probably won't be long. You can wait for him out here if you want.
BILL. I'll just leave them if that's all right.

MARY. That's fine. Put them anywhere on the porch.

BILL. Are you Mrs. Ellis?

MARY. I am. And you must be Mr. Riddick.

BILL. How did you know?

MARY. Because no Negro in this town would show up at this door carrying just a box of paper.

BILL. *(Smiles.)* Will we see you at the charrette?

MARY. No, I'm afraid not.

BILL. Do you mind if I ask why?

MARY. Well, in the long run I don't see showing up matters much.

BILL. Really. Have you lived here long?

MARY. All my life.

BILL. And you don't think race relations are a problem?

MARY. To me, race relations are just the tip of the iceberg, Mr. Riddick.

BILL. Why would you say that?

MARY. Black, white; those are just skin colors. I think there's a lot more to it than that. I think there's something inside us, every one of us that freezes up, when we see anybody different. It's like a gate that slams down so we can feel safe behind it. Not just when it's about black or white, but when it's about religion or pretty much anything you can think of. I'll bet you're a Democrat?

BILL. You'd bet right.

MARY. I'm a Republican. There's another line right there. How many people do you know who cross it? And even if we got rid of every line we'd probably go starting wars between who's right–handed or left–handed.

BILL. Isn't that a sad way to look at the world, Mrs. Ellis?

MARY. No. It doesn't stop you from doing everything you can for your family or anybody who you think you can really help. But you don't waste time fooling yourself you can push a boulder up a mountain. You just try to keep it from rolling back down on you. *(Sound of a cry offstage: It's hard to understand, sounds like "Maaaaa.")* Excuse me. That's my son. Now, he's worth fighting for. *(Lights down on Mary and Bill. Sound of shop doorbell ringing. Lights up on Jake's Appliances. C.P. enters, holding surveys.)*

C.P. Hot as hell out there, Jake; your air conditioners should be selling themselves. I want you to fill out one of these surveys about our schools. You can write, can't you? Give our side of the story.

(Pause, C.P. loses his smile.) Who told you that? Legman? That man's so stupid he could throw himself on the ground and miss. *(Lights up on Ann in high school addressing students.)*

ANN. Settle down! I appreciate you children staying after school like this. I just read your surveys and there's some things I'd like to talk about.

C.P. That was horse trading! They brought in their choir and we got our Klan exhibit. *(Pause.)* Of course I went to see 'em sing, I had to! I'm the co-chair for Christ's sake! *(Lights up on Bill's hotel room, Bill arguing on the phone with his supervisor.)*

BILL. So they had a Klan exhibit! Nobody got hurt, did they? The church choir didn't start a riot either!

C.P. Legman can call me any damn name he wants, but I haven't seen him at the charrette even once to say it to my face like a man. Haven't seen you there either. Fill it out or don't, Jake. Not for nothing, your opinion don't mean shit to me. *(Lights out on C.P. as he walks out.)*

BILL. You think you can do a better job than me, then get yourself down here! You've got eight days left to do it! *(Pause.)* There's only two things that can happen. We're either going to tear this town apart or do some real mending. *(Lights down on Bill.)*

ANN. You say the whites' schools have better teachers, bigger sports programs, and they send more of theirs to college. Then you say there's no way you'd sit in the same classrooms as white kids. And I got a lot of answers like this one, saying that what you really want to do is what they did to us: burn their school down. *(Lights down on Ann. Lights up on C.P. walking down the street. He stops, spotting someone, waves.)*

C.P. Councilman Nash! Ferris! *(He stops. C.P. watches as Councilman Nash crosses the street to avoid him. C.P. slowly puts his hand down.)* Son of a bitch. *(Lights down on C.P. Darkness in C.P. and Mary's kitchen. A tongue of light as a match is lit; Mary is smoking a cigarette. C.P. enters. He's had more than a few drinks.)* Don't even say it. I've been drinking. *(He turns on a light. Mary sits with a drink and bottle and glass beside her.)*

MARY. So have I. You want one?

C.P. *(Surprised.)* Okay. *(She pours.)* You going to tell me what's going on here?

MARY. Looks like you're the one upset.

C.P. I saw Ferris Nash today, "Councilman" Ferris, coming down the boulevard. I called to him and he turns on that big cheese grin of his 'til he saw it was me. Then he crossed the street. My "good friend" crossed the street because he didn't want to be seen with me.

MARY. You don't understand that?

C.P. Hell no! That bastard's called me a dozen times to get us out to protests and demonstrations to say what he won't and do what he's afraid to!

MARY. That's why he's a politician.

C.P. He's a lying backstabber.

MARY. That's why he's a politician.

C.P. I'm taking hell for this town and they're chewing my ass ragged! Well, no more. The hell with them and this damn charrette!

MARY. So you're quitting now?

C.P. What do you care? Really? You won't join the Klan; you don't go to the charrette. Damn it, Mary, what am I supposed to tell folks? You make me look like a fool! My own wife won't support me.

MARY. I'm still here, C.P. That's supporting you.

C.P. It's not enough. *(Pause.)*

MARY. I went to the doctor today.

C.P. What's wrong with Larry now?

MARY. I didn't go for Larry. I went for me.

C.P. Why?

MARY. I've had some trouble breathing. So I went to see Dr. Miller last week.

C.P. What did he say?

MARY. He sent me to a specialist, at the hospital. He wanted a second opinion.

C.P. Second opinion about what? Mary?

MARY. I'm going to tell you. But I need you to be strong. Just listen and think before you say a word. Because I don't know if you can deal with this. And if you can't, I need to know now.

C.P. Go on. Tell me. *(Lights down on C.P. and Mary. Lights up on school auditorium. Ann walks in and sits, exhausted. C.P. enters moments later.)*

ANN. You're here early.

C.P. You got a problem with that? You're here early yourself.

ANN. I don't set the bus schedule.

C.P. We got to start this meeting on time tonight. Get home at a decent hour.

ANN. Tell me about it. I've got to go find planets. My daughter Lydia's got to make a solar system. *(Pause. C.P. fills the silence.)*

C.P. How many kids you got?

ANN. Two girls. You?

C.P. Two sons. One daughter.

ANN. How many are still talking to you?

C.P. What's that mean?

ANN. My girls get madder at me every day. Marilyn, she's a sophomore, the kids are at her 'cause her mother's working with a Klansman. Lydia's friends say she's got a big head, just like me, since my name's in the paper. They're mad 'cause they're scared. And all they've got is me to be mad at.

C.P. *(Pause.)* Ain't that something.

ANN. That's something all right.

C.P. My boy Tim, he's been getting in a lot of fights. Kids say, "Your daddy sold us down the river." Vickie, my girl, picked up the phone a few nights back — somebody cussing me down, foul talk. Foul. She was so scared she couldn't sleep. Still can't. *(Pause.)*

ANN. You read the surveys?

C.P. Yeah.

ANN. Got a lot of hate here.

C.P. That surprise you?

ANN. What surprised me was hearing how the teachers treat the kids.

C.P. Here we go. The black kids, right?

ANN. The poor kids. Black or white. Every time there's some problem or a fight, it's always the fault of the kid whose parents don't have two nickels to rub together. Lydia, she forgot her homework and the teacher called her a liar, said she never did it. Same day, a boy in her class whose daddy's a bigshot at the Mutual forgets his, and the teacher didn't bat an eye, just told him to bring it tomorrow.

C.P. You mean the Mutual Insurance? I thought they were your people.

ANN. They might have been black when they started up, but nowadays the only color they care about is green. They look down at the rest of us like we're not worth selling insurance to.

C.P. My son heard his science teacher tell the principal that the kids who get the bad grades are the "poor white trash" who can't do better. Tim didn't tell me for two days, he was so ashamed. I sat him down; I told him money doesn't matter, but he knows I'm lying.

ANN. I tell my girls they're just as good as anybody else. Anybody. Then they go to school and see girls wearing new dresses and shoes and think, "Who does she think she's fooling?"

C.P. My kids got more than I ever did, I'll tell you that. And they should appreciate it. I grew up north of the tracks, you know those houses. Hell, shacks. Some families shared an outhouse. I'd be lucky to have a lunch to bring to school. I'd wait for the rest of the kids to eat theirs and go play so they wouldn't see me eating my biscuit and lard. They'd say, "How's your sandwich, linthead?" That's what they called us, "lintheads;" all the kids whose daddies worked the mill.

ANN. You got a violin? 'Cause I can't play it.

C.P. I don't want your sympathy, Atwater.

ANN. Good.

C.P. I'm breaking my back for my kids! They've got food on the table, a backyard, and our own driveway. I open my station at 5:00 every morning and they should appreciate it.

ANN. Maybe you should appreciate having your own business.

C.P. Who says I don't? What do you do?

ANN. I worked for a lady down on Beacon.

C.P. "Worked"? She fire you?

ANN. I quit. I've been out looking for a new job every day the last three weeks now.

C.P. What was wrong with your old job?

ANN. The job was fine. I worked there coming on seven years. Did her wash and ironing, cleaned, cooked lunch and I made dinner too. She didn't pay for me for that, but sometimes she let me take home leftovers.

C.P. A white woman?

ANN. Of course a white woman.

C.P. So why would you go and quit?

ANN. *(Not sure if she wants to tell him.)* I was in the laundry room folding clothes. I heard her and her friend having tea in the kitchen talking about bussing. Not that they ever ride one. Her friend says, "I just don't understand it. As long as they get a seat, what's so special about sitting up front?" That set me off. I've shut my mouth ten thousand times, but somehow this just set me off. I charged out of there and started shouting in their faces about justice and God and Divine Retribution. I told them they'd burn in hell and I'd light the match. I can't even remember if I quit or I was fired.

And it took me 'til I was halfway home to realize what I did to my children. No more money, food, no second–hand clothes. And you can call me crazy, but if I had quit a month ago, before this charrette? I swear I would have found a new job in two days. But now? Folks recognize me. "That's her. The one stirring things up."

C.P. I tell ya. People aren't coming into my station. Gas, repairs. I used to have more than I could handle. Now they drive by and don't even turn their heads. Customers I've had for years. Friends. You know what folks tell my kids? Your daddy's a white nigger. *(Ann usually looked at him here.)* That's right. People lookin' down at me like I'm no better than you. *(C.P. stops, seeing Ann's reaction at hearing him. For the first time, he's heard himself.)*

C.P. Sorry.

ANN. Sorry? You're sorry? Tell me, what exactly are you sorry for? For what you just said? That's nothing. How about for what you are and what you've always been. Don't you worry about sorry with me. You just be sorry for your own damn self. *(Lights down on C.P. Lights up on Ann. She's sitting, speaking with her pastor. In the background we hear the sound of someone practicing a hymn on the church organ. A mistake, they start again. Lights down. Lights up reveal Mary at Ann's front door. Mary is carrying a bag.)*

MARY. Mrs. Atwater? I'm Mary Ellis.

ANN. C.P.'s wife?

MARY. That's right.

ANN. I'd have never believed it.

MARY. What?

ANN. How that man could end up with a woman pretty as you?

MARY. That's very kind.

ANN. No. That's the truth. What can I do for you?

MARY. Would you mind inviting me inside for a minute?

ANN. This neighborhood make you nervous?

MARY. Actually, it's the sun. I need to get off my feet for a minute. But that's all right, I'd best go.

ANN. Come on in.

MARY. Thank you.

ANN. It's not that I have much reputation left. *(She reenters holding the bag.)*

MARY. You've got a nice place here.

ANN. It's clean. Go ahead and sit. Does C.P. know you're here?

MARY. No. And I'd like to keep it that way if you don't mind.

ANN. I don't mind. Believe me, I'm done small talking with that man.

MARY. That's a shame.

ANN. Why?

MARY. Sometimes that's the only way he knows how to talk.

ANN. Maybe it'd be better if he just kept his mouth shut.

MARY. I can't tell you how many times I thought the same thing. But at least I never have to guess what he's thinking. Some people just smile back at you and you never know. Those are the ones I don't trust.

ANN. They're all the same to me. I don't waste time separating them out. I just don't trust anybody.

MARY. Your daughter Lydia works at the post office with my Vickie.

ANN. Is that right.

MARY. Vickie says they haven't talked since this whole business started.

ANN. *(Surprised.)* They talked before that?

MARY. They did.

ANN. Did Lydia always know your girl's C.P.'s daughter?

MARY. Yes.

ANN. And they still talked?

MARY. That's right. She knows Vickie is my daughter, too. I suppose she "separates" us out. *(Ann smiles.)*

ANN. I've got iced tea, would you like some?

MARY. I'd like that very much. *(Blackout. Onscreen footage of reporters interviewing members of a town council.)*

CHARLIE LANG. *(Voiceover.)* Good Morning, Durham. Don't know if you were there at last night's charrette, but I hear half the city was. Me, I'm staying in and locking my doors, because we've been invaded. Reporters, TV cameras, photographers; we've got more Yankees down here now than when we were fighting the War. So what's today's battle? I say it's C.P. Ellis and Ann Atwater meeting the town Council and the School Board, and I'll betcha it's going to be a battle bloodier than Antietam. This is Charlie Lang, WBDK, the voice of Durham. *(Lights up reveal Ann, C.P. and Bill, going over a thick report. C.P. seems as out of sorts as he did days earlier at Ruth's Café.)*

BILL. You've got a lot here to present. Who's going to lead off? *(C.P. is silent. Ann looks at him.)*

ANN. I will.

BILL. C.P.?

C.P. Doesn't matter to me.

BILL. It's a closed session, so at least you won't have the press at you.

C.P. *(Gets up.)* Is that it?

BILL. I was hoping we could review your main points before the Council and School Board get here. *(C.P. looks at his watch, reluctantly sits.)* You're recommending that students should have a say in how the schools are run.

ANN. Four students on the School Board. Two black, two white.

BILL. *(Referring to the report.)* That schools should provide individual instruction to students who need it. And the same textbooks and curriculum should be used in every classroom.

ANN. With books that have black faces in them.

BILL. *(Looks to C.P., who is still silent, impatient.)* C.P.?

C.P. That's what the committee voted for.

BILL. *(Takes note of C.P.'s attitude.)* You've got a lot of bold ideas here. But I want to be clear about your last point. You say there should be procedures in place to deal with racial violence in the schools.

ANN. That's right.

BILL. What you're not saying is what that implies. You don't need procedures for violence if black and white students aren't in the same schools. You're endorsing integration.

ANN. We're endorsing the law. It's time this city opens its eyes wide enough to see tomorrow.

BILL. You back all this?

C.P. I don't back a damn thing. I did my job, didn't I? I passed out the surveys, organized the meetings and took down what everybody decided.

BILL. I'm asking if you agree with these findings.

C.P. *(Gets up again.)* I don't have to, do I? I've got to drive my wife to an appointment. I'll be here at two.

BILL. See you then. *(C.P. leaves without another word. Bill turns to Ann.)* We've got over a thousand of people at the Duke Hotel tonight. It's supposed to be a celebration.

ANN. You have a problem with our report?

BILL. The problem is C.P. He was like a bomb ticking. What's he thinking?

ANN. How should I know? I'm not getting inside that head.

BILL. Usually at the end of a charrette we ask the chairpersons to make closing speeches. In this case I'm not sure that would be a good idea. He could wipe out all the good work we've done with one comment.

ANN. So to keep his mouth shut you want me to shut mine, too.

BILL. You think I'm wrong?

ANN. I think that leaves you the only one making speeches.

BILL. I'll be short and sweet.

ANN. Do tell. Riddick, you're a rooster. Like my daddy used to say, you think the sun comes up just to hear you crow.

BILL. You know, sometimes I can't tell who you dislike more, C.P. or me?

ANN. Sometimes a horse race ends in a dead heat.

BILL. Are you married?

ANN. That's none of your business.

BILL. It's just that you call yourself "Mrs. Atwater" and I've never met your husband.

ANN. You'd have to find him first.

BILL. Then I guess it's safe to say you're not a fan of men in general.

ANN. Only the ones I met.

BILL. Then why'd you ever get married?

ANN. Because I was pregnant. And because my daddy brought his gun to the wedding.

BILL. That would do it.

ANN. My daddy was a deacon in our church. He told me I had to follow my husband to Durham like a wife should. Especially when he promised he'd find a job here.

BILL. He didn't?

ANN. He did. If you count on selling whiskey out of his boardinghouse.

BILL. It must have been hard.

ANN. Don't you go pitying me. Don't you dare. A woman who can't take care of herself is as worthless as the man who makes her feel that way.

BILL. "Roughhouse Annie."

ANN. Back then's when I got the name. One night my husband told me I was being too friendly with the men who bought his liquor, said not to talk to them. I told him I'd talk to whoever I wanted. He slapped me across the face, knocked me back into the woodstove. But I grabbed the ax. I picked it up and swung and he jumped back, fell through the back door, glass flying everywhere. Then I got the police.

BILL. They arrested him?

36

ANN. They would have. But he talked me out of pressing charges. Said he'd never be able to get a job to support us. And I believed him. He took every penny I had, lit off to Richmond and left me pregnant with my second daughter. I never met a man I could trust, Riddick, so don't feel special, you're just one more of 'em.

BILL. I'm getting married in three weeks.

ANN. Really? I never met your bride.

BILL. You won't, either. One talk with you and she'd be the one grabbing an ax. *(Lights down on Bill and Ann. Lights up in the hospital waiting room. C.P. is sitting. Mary emerges from the doctor's office.)*

MARY. The doctor will call us in once he reads the x-rays. You want a magazine or something?

C.P. These guys always keep you waiting. Like they're saying our time's not worth a thing compared to theirs.

MARY. When you get home tonight we've got to talk. We've got to decide what to do about Larry. He's getting too big to take care of. Even if it was both of us.

C.P. It will be. I don't want to hear otherwise.

MARY. It's not about you. It's about what's best for him. Finding someplace that can help him more than we can. *(Pause.)* Then there's Timmy and Vickie. We've got to think about them, too.

C.P. There's nothing to think about! You'll take care of them the same you do now! And I'll keep them in line, you can count on that.

MARY. We can't count on anything. Things are going to change.

C.P. No.

MARY. I know you hate change. But things don't stay the same.

C.P. Some do.

MARY. Name one thing.

C.P. You.

MARY. You are so wrong.

C.P. You think so. But you're still with me, aren't you?

MARY. Maybe it's because I don't have the strength to run.

C.P. There's that. You ran after me fast enough when you first saw me playing baseball.

MARY. I liked baseball.

C.P. That's not all you liked.

MARY. What about you? Coming into Woolworth's every time you had money for your ice cream sodas?

C.P. I liked my sodas. And the girl who made them. Who is just as pretty now as she was back then. That's never changed, either.

MARY. Stop. *(Pause.)* No, never mind. Keep it up.

C.P. You're going to get better. And if this doctor can't help you, we'll find you one who can. I'm not giving up, Mary. I promise you that.

MARY. Promise me this. We're not going to be here in fifty years, neither of us. But our kids will be. And their kids. Put them first, C.P. Always put them first. *(She takes his arm. Lights down on doctor's office. Lights up on City Council chamber. Both Ann and C.P. are at podiums. C.P. has a stack of reports. Bill sits by their side.)*

FERRIS. Mrs. Atwater, you've made a lot of very interesting points. All of us on the Council and the School Board want to thank you, Mr. Ellis and your charrette for all the fine work you've done. We're going to organize a committee to study your report and give it all due consideration.

ANN. "Due consideration"? What does that mean? There are things you can work on right now. Like replacing the teachers in our black schools teaching subjects they never trained for. English teachers teaching math. Gym teachers teaching science. How are children going to learn by that? And another thing, you can talk to all the principals right now and find out why it is that when a black student gets caught selling drugs, they call the police, but when it's a white kid, they call his parents. Mr. Ellis heard this the same as I did. *(C.P. says nothing; will he back her up?)* C.P.? Do you have anything to say?

FERRIS. I'm sure he does. Mr. Ellis has always been an outstanding public servant. C.P., why don't you explain to Mrs. Atwater, on your way out, that we're going to do all we can. We will now go into a private session. Thank you both.

C.P. I know you're gonna do all you can. Because we put a lot of hours into this charrette. And because I'm giving copies of our report to all those reporters outside and I know they'll read them real fast. Not as fast as you, of course, considering our past history together, fraternal organizations and such. Boys, fellow "public servants," it's your turn, now. Ferris? I'll see you around town. *(C.P. picks up reports and hands half his pile to Ann, who is surprised.)* Here's yours. Let's do this thing. *(Lights down on Council chambers, lights up on Duke Hotel. Sound of music being played and the celebratory crowd at the charrette's closing party. Lights up on C.P., a drink in his hand. He's dressed in a tie for the first time. He's alone. And feels it. Bill approaches, also with a drink.)*

BILL. Good turnout.

C.P. Yep.

BILL. Today's the first time I ever saw a roomful of jaws hit the ground at once. They're going to move on this, C.P. You didn't give them a choice.

C.P. Maybe.

BILL. I hope you're proud of what you did here.

C.P. *(Shrugging it off.)* What's done is done.

BILL. It's not done. Not even close.

C.P. It is for me.

BILL. *(Uncomfortable.)* C.P.? Some of the Committee thought it would be a nice gesture if the co-chairs had a dance together.

C.P. I'm not dancing with her. No way.

BILL. That's fine. I'll go tell them. *(He starts to go.)*

C.P. I'll drink a toast with her.

BILL. A toast? *(Reluctant.)* All right. *(Bill gets the microphone. C.P. downs his drink.)* If I can have everybody's attention … Can we turn the music off? *(Music stops.)* Thank you. Ann, will you join us to make a toast? Everybody else, get a drink in your hand if you've been too slow to grab one already. *(Ann arrives, drink in hand. Bill introduces her.)* Ann Atwater, our co-chair. *(Bill steps aside for her to use the mic.)*

ANN. Here's to our charrette! What we've done and what we've still got to do. *(Ann raises her glass; strong applause.)*

BILL. C.P.?

C.P. *(Bill puts the microphone in front of him.)* I hope it did some good. *(Applause; everyone drains their glasses.)*

BILL. *(Pulls microphone away.)* Thank you. Congratulations to all of you who worked so hard —

C.P. I'm not done yet. *(Reluctantly, Bill hands C.P. the microphone.)* I'm looking out at all of you. Most of you folks I haven't talked to my entire life, and a lot of you never talked to me. Maybe still won't. I'd be lying if I didn't say this whole thing wasn't hell. It was. Especially spending it with Ann Atwater. I always thought she was the meanest black woman God put on this earth. I knew I was better than her. Turns out what I didn't know is that she's somebody trying to help her people the same as I'm trying to help mine. People who don't have much. Lower class. I figured out this much. Folks don't stay upper class unless the rest of us are underneath them. And as long as we keep fighting each other they know we're going to leave them alone to run things the way they always have, looking out for themselves and nobody else. And that's not right. It's not right. I've been a proud member of the Ku Klux Klan since I was twenty-three years old. *(Takes out his wallet and his card.)* This is my membership card. Exalted Cyclops of Durham Klavern, Unit 9. After this charrette, will our schools really get better? I don't know. What I do know is that most of us in this room aren't going to be around in fifty years. But our kids will be. And their kids. So, for things to get better, something has to change. We've got to put our children first. *(C.P. rips up his card.)* That's all I've got to say. *(C.P. leaves. The audience is stunned, as are Bill and Ann.)*

BILL. I don't believe it. Did you see what that man did? I'm going to get him. We need a picture.

ANN. No. No. Let him be. *(Music concludes as we fade to black; lights up on church cross. Sound of reverend's voice.)*

REVEREND. *(Voiceover.)* We ask you, Father, to welcome your servant Mary Ellis into heaven. We thank you that her suffering here on earth was short. And we pray for her soul and the souls of all of our dearly departed and for the family Mary left behind.

ALL. *(Voiceover.)* Amen. *(Lights up on C.P.'s kitchen. He's on the phone, wearing his t-shirt, with two six–packs of beer, empty, and a nearly–finished bottle of whiskey on the table. He puts down the can opener he opens the last beer with.)*

C.P. Denny, C.P. … Yeah, I appreciate that … When we found out it was too late. It kept spreading, no matter what. But she fought like hell, you know Mary, she fought hard, but, listen, Denny, I've still got my keys to the Klavern. I thought maybe I could come over and drop them off … Sure. I can mail 'em. Wait! I've been writing this letter. I want to explain to the boys why I did what I did, I thought maybe you could read it at a meeting so they'd understand … Sure. You go on and eat. Talk later. *(C.P. hangs up the phone, takes a drink, then dials again.)* Clayton, this is C.P. How's the fam — *(Sound of a hangup. C.P. gets up, paces the room. He stops before the living room wall, stands, stares at it. Suddenly C.P. punches through the plasterboard. Again. Again. He goes back to his chair, drinks from the bottle, then picks up the can opener. He hikes one long sleeve up, the back of his hand to the audience, and draws can opener across his wrist. He puts his hand down and we see the cut and blood. Blackout. Sound of ambulance. Lights up on John Umstead hospital. Ann stands before a nurse's station.)*

ANN. Nurse? *(She waits and is ignored.)* NURSE! I see you back

40

there. *(Nurse emerges.)* Can you tell me what room C.P. Ellis is at? *(She looks at her watch.)* It's only three-fifty; visiting hours end at four o'clock. *(Nurse tells her to come back tomorrow.)* I am not coming back, I've got ten minutes left to visit and I'm seeing him now. *(She starts to go, then turns back at the nurse's comment.)* You go on, you call security. Call the army, too, 'cause it's going to take all of them to budge me. *(Lights up on C.P. He's seated, wearing a bathrobe, bandages on his wrist. Ann enters.)* C.P. *(C.P. stands. Neither knows if they should shake hands or embrace, so they do neither. C.P. can't look at her.)*

C.P. I didn't think anybody knew I was here. Things have been quiet, you know? Nobody's come. Sit down, go on. You want some Jell-O? They keep bringing me Jell-O. I can't stand the stuff. Especially when it's green or orange. Blue, once. Sometimes it's got little fruit pieces trapped inside. Makes it even worse. Who'd even think of inventing something that's nothing but water and dye and cow hooves? Useless. Absolutely useless.

ANN. I'm sorry to hear about your wife. I was in Charlotte. I didn't know 'til I got back.

C.P. Don't know how she put up with me. The way she kept us in line; Mary could have run the world from the kitchen as long as she had her cup of coffee and a cigarette. She was a good woman.

ANN. She was. *(C.P. looks at her.)* My Marilyn worked with your daughter Vickie after school at the phone company. They got to talking. When I was out of work, Mary brought me vegetables from her garden. Brought me fatback, too. Some nights that was all we had to eat.

C.P. She never told me that. *(Pause.)* She hated me being in the Klan. Said it was because I was away from home too much, but I knew it was more than that. Remember my gun?

ANN. How could I forget your gun?

C.P. She buried it in cement. Filled up the trunk of my car and buried it. Thought I was going to kill somebody. I almost did, once. *(Uncomfortable silence.)*

ANN. So did I. I sure wanted to. If somebody didn't stop me I would have killed him for sure.

C.P. Who was that?

ANN. You. *(Pause.)* You remember the Housing Projects hearings maybe two years back? We had broken windows, rats, no wa-

41

ter. I had a bathtub that fell through my floor. Landlord wouldn't fix a thing. Even when we got a lawyer he'd get extension after extension from the mayor. You were there at the last hearing. When our lawyer told the Council that animals lived better, you got up and said we were worse than animals. Niggers wouldn't know how to keep their homes decent anyways. You were standing in the row right in front of me with your "nigger" this and "nigger" that. So I got out the pocketknife I kept in my handbag and opened the blade. The next "nigger" I heard I jumped up with my knife in my hand to cut your throat ear to ear, grab your hair and cut so deep I could watch you bleed out right in front of me. Pastor Walker saw that knife and pulled me down hard. Don't do it, he told me. Don't give them the satisfaction. I had as much hate in me as you did, maybe more. I knew it, but I couldn't let it go. It was so strong I thought if I let it go there'd be nothing left of me. *(Pause.)* I'm asking if you can forgive me.

C.P. Yeah. I guess I can. *(Pause.)* You know what I keep thinking? I miss the Klan. It makes no sense, but … you don't want to hear this.

ANN. Go on.

C.P. The night they swore me in was the greatest moment in my life. I got down on one knee before the Altar. Everybody looking at me take the oath before our leader. "By the fiery cross I dedicate you, Claiborne Paul Ellis, in the holy service of our country, our Klan, our families and each other." The whole room clapped for me; hundreds of them; nobody ever clapped for me before. I was part of something. I was somebody.

ANN. You still are.

C.P. Me? I'm a janitor now, you know that? Lucky to get the job when I lost the station. It's a funny thing. My old friends won't talk to me. Those new white folks I met at the charrette, I can't talk to them, I'm not educated like they are.

ANN. You know the terrible thing we did, C.P.? We changed. If people think that's a crime, then let them. They're wrong and we're right. Your life's not over, just your old one. You've got to get on with the new one. *(C.P. looks at Ann, then looks down.)*

C.P. I can't dance. That's why I said no.

ANN. *What?*

C.P. That last night of the charrette, that's why I wouldn't dance with you. I don't know how.

ANN. You don't know how to keep time clapping to the music,

either.

C.P. What?

ANN. You clap off the beat. *(Demonstrates as she sings a small bit of a song. C.P. smiles.)* You ever come to church with me some Sunday and I'll teach you how.

C.P. You watch out, maybe someday I will.

ANN. Invitation's open. *(Ann smiles at him. It's hard to tell who moves toward the other first. Ann hugs C.P.; C.P. embraces her with all his strength. Both are overwhelmed. They rock back and forth. Almost dancing.)*

ANN. It's okay. It's okay. *(Sound of microphone static, a crowd in the background. Lights up on a banner that reads, "Local 465 International Union of Operating Engineers.")*

ANNOUNCER. Thanks you, Mr. Rice. We'll hear now from the next candidate for Chief Steward, Mr. C.P. Ellis. *(Light applause. C.P. steps into the light; he is wearing his janitor's uniform.)*

C.P. I've been a member of this union almost five years now, but I guess most of you don't know me because of that. Some of you say I'm crazy to even think of running for Steward when 90% of you are black. Maybe I am. Or maybe I'm just not used to being a minority. But I wasn't thinking like a white man when I decided I wanted to throw my hat in. I was thinking like a man who lost his house because he couldn't make payments. A man who people look right through when he's wearing a janitor's uniform, like he's not there. A man who does honest work and deserves an honest shake on payday. That's the man I'd represent. So if you can look past who I was, I'll tell you who I'll be: Somebody who will fight for you, somebody you can count on to keep their word. Somebody who would be proud to represent you. *(Sound of applause that, to C.P.'s surprise, builds.)*

RADIO ANNOUNCER. C.P. Ellis, former Ku Klux Klan leader, died this week in North Carolina. Ellis was well known for co-chairing community efforts to desegregate Durham schools nearly twenty-five years ago. He was later elected Chief Steward of the Local 465 Union of Operating Engineers and spent eighteen years organizing union workers throughout North Carolina. Services will be held for him on Friday at Durham's Christ Church. *(Pre-service organ music is heard. Lights up on Ann as Bill Riddick and Ann enter.)*

ANN. Bill Riddick. I haven't seen you since the charrette.

BILL. How are you, Ann?

ANN. I'm fine. How about yourself?

BILL. I'm good. Good. Three children and seven grandchildren.

ANN. You still married?

BILL. Even to the same woman.

ANN. How about that.

BILL. *(Uncomfortable.)* It shouldn't have taken a funeral to get me back here. I should have been back to see both of you a long time ago. The charrette led to a lot of good things for me. Jobs, speaking engagements. It raised my family. But I never kept in contact. I didn't know how strapped you and C.P. were.

ANN. We got by.

BILL. I'm sorry. I've been blessed and I didn't share it. I used to think I was some kind of genius getting you both to be the charrette's co-chairs. When I look back on the night C.P. tore up his KKK card, I still can't believe it. Out of my children being born, it was the most important night of my life.

ANN. It was a miracle.

BILL. I thought it was me. I don't think that anymore.

ANN. You're not so cocky now, either. That's another miracle.

BILL. It's a funny thing; you get older, you look around you and see what's changed and what hasn't. Sure, laws have changed, there's more opportunity, and now people don't say what they're really feeling to your face. But still … I met Mary Ellis once. She thought people couldn't change, not down deep where it matters. There are lines that never go away. Maybe she was right. I want to have hope. But it's getting harder. *(Music changes.)*

ANN. The service is starting. Don't you go anywhere. *(Lights up on podium, Ann steps up to it.)* I'm proud that C.P.'s family invited me to speak today at his funeral. We knew each other a long time now. C.P. helped me when my roof was about to fall in. I helped him get his son Larry into a place he gets good care. We helped each other when one of us needed anything, whether it was money or a meal or just company. C.P. lost a lot of his old friends. Most of them. He could have left town, but he stayed. He said this was his home and that was that. You know, when C.P. was the head of the Local 465 he organized their first paid holiday on Martin Luther King Day. A lot of white men went after him for that, but C.P. told them, "Okay, fool, you don't like it, then go on in and work that day." We got a good laugh out of that. I believe God had a plan for both of us, for C.P. and for me to learn to work together. Well, we did. C.P.

Ellis was my friend. He was a good man, and I trusted him. Way back when we worked on the charrette here, the man who brought us all together, Bill Riddick, told us he wasn't hoping for a mile of change, just an inch. I thought of that yesterday when I went to the funeral parlor. I was looking for a place to sit when this white man looked up and says, "This wake's for Claiborne Ellis." I told him I knew. He says, "I'm sorry, but it's for family members only." I said I know that, too. He said to me, "Well, are you a family member?" I said, "Yes, I am. C.P. is my brother." He stared at me, I stared at him, then he slid over on the bench so I could sit. Not much. Just a few inches. But it was enough. *(Lights fade to black. Music heard as actors take their bows. Hymn: "I'm Going with Jesus.")*
CHOIR.

I'm going with Jesus all the way
I'm going with Jesus all the way
You can't stop me, you can't turn me
I'm going with Jesus all the way
Sometimes I have to fast and pray
Sometimes I have to steal away
Sometimes I have to cry out help me Lord
(Oh yes.)
I know if I hold my peace, the Lord will
Take care of me
I'm going to Jesus all the way
If you need Him, just clap your hands
(A little louder.)
Come on and just clap your hands
(A little louder.)
I'm going, with Jesus
I'm going, with Jesus
I'm going, with Jesus

End of Play

PROPERTY LIST

Beer
Flyers
Oil rag
Tire iron
Phones
Klan banner
Pocketbook
Machine gun
3 plates of food
Wallet, cash
Cup of coffee
Cigarette
Empty bourbon bottle
Stack of papers
Stapler
Clipboard
Notes
Flyer
Box of surveys
Matches
Bag
Report
Stack of reports
Drinks
Microphone
Wallet, KKK membership card
2 six-packs of beer, empty
Nearly empty bottle of whiskey
Can opener

SOUND EFFECTS

Cheering crowd, blends with protest-crowd chant
Car driving into gas station, ring of gas-station line
Radio announcer
Phone ring
Restaurant noice and 1971 music hit
Door opening and closing
Jesse Helms voiceover
School bell
Classes changing
Political ad voiceover
Teeh voices
Louder murmering
Song on Radio
"I'm going with Jesus" Gospel hum
Shop door bell
Church organ practising a hymn; mistake, start over
Voice over, City Council meeting
Music and celebratory party
Voice over, Reverend's voice
Phone hangup
Ambulance
Microphone static
Announcer
Applause
Radio Announcer
Organ music

NEW PLAYS

★ **CLYBOURNE PARK by Bruce Norris.** WINNER OF THE 2011 PULITZER PRIZE AND 2012 TONY AWARD. Act One takes place in 1959 as community leaders try to stop the sale of a home to a black family. Act Two is set in the same house in the present day as the now predominantly African-American neighborhood battles to hold its ground. "Vital, sharp-witted and ferociously smart." *–NY Times.* "A theatrical treasure…Indisputably, uproariously funny." *–Entertainment Weekly.* [4M, 3W] ISBN: 978-0-8222-2697-0

★ **WATER BY THE SPOONFUL by Quiara Alegría Hudes.** WINNER OF THE 2012 PULITZER PRIZE. A Puerto Rican veteran is surrounded by the North Philadelphia demons he tried to escape in the service. "This is a very funny, warm, and yes uplifting play." *–Hartford Courant.* "The play is a combination poem, prayer and app on how to cope in an age of uncertainty, speed and chaos." *–Variety.* [4M, 3W] ISBN: 978-0-8222-2716-8

★ **RED by John Logan.** WINNER OF THE 2010 TONY AWARD. Mark Rothko has just landed the biggest commission in the history of modern art. But when his young assistant, Ken, gains the confidence to challenge him, Rothko faces the agonizing possibility that his crowning achievement could also become his undoing. "Intense and exciting." *–NY Times.* "Smart, eloquent entertainment." *–New Yorker.* [2M] ISBN: 978-0-8222-2483-9

★ **VENUS IN FUR by David Ives.** Thomas, a beleaguered playwright/director, is desperate to find an actress to play Vanda, the female lead in his adaptation of the classic sadomasochistic tale *Venus in Fur.* "Ninety minutes of good, kinky fun." *–NY Times.* "A fast-paced journey into one man's entrapment by a clever, vengeful female." *–Associated Press.* [1M, 1W] ISBN: 978-0-8222-2603-1

★ **OTHER DESERT CITIES by Jon Robin Baitz.** Brooke returns home to Palm Springs after a six-year absence and announces that she is about to publish a memoir dredging up a pivotal and tragic event in the family's history—a wound they don't want reopened. "Leaves you feeling both moved and gratifyingly sated." *–NY Times.* "A genuine pleasure." *–NY Post.* [2M, 3W] ISBN: 978-0-8222-2605-5

★ **TRIBES by Nina Raine.** Billy was born deaf into a hearing family and adapts brilliantly to his family's unconventional ways, but it's not until he meets Sylvia, a young woman on the brink of deafness, that he finally understands what it means to be understood. "A smart, lively play." *–NY Times.* "[A] bright and boldly provocative drama." *–Associated Press.* [3M, 2W] ISBN: 978-0-8222-2751-9

DRAMATISTS PLAY SERVICE, INC.
440 Park Avenue South, New York, NY 10016 212-683-8960 Fax 212-213-1539
postmaster@dramatists.com www.dramatists.com